AF264269

Dedication

To my family & friends who helped bring these playful animals to life — thank you for inspiring me & sharing in the fun of creating them!

To everyone, may this book bring as much joy to you as creating it did to me.

About the Author

Balancing a career of service with a passion for creativity, Rachel McNeil is an active-duty member of the United States Coast Guard and the artist behind this coloring book. A psychology graduate with a lifelong passion for art, Rachel sketched each illustration for this book, imagining whimsical transformations with the help of her friends and family. She enjoys reading, playing with her Frenchie (Buoy), and going to the beach in her free time. Rachel grew up in the small town of Sedley, VA with her parents and sister.

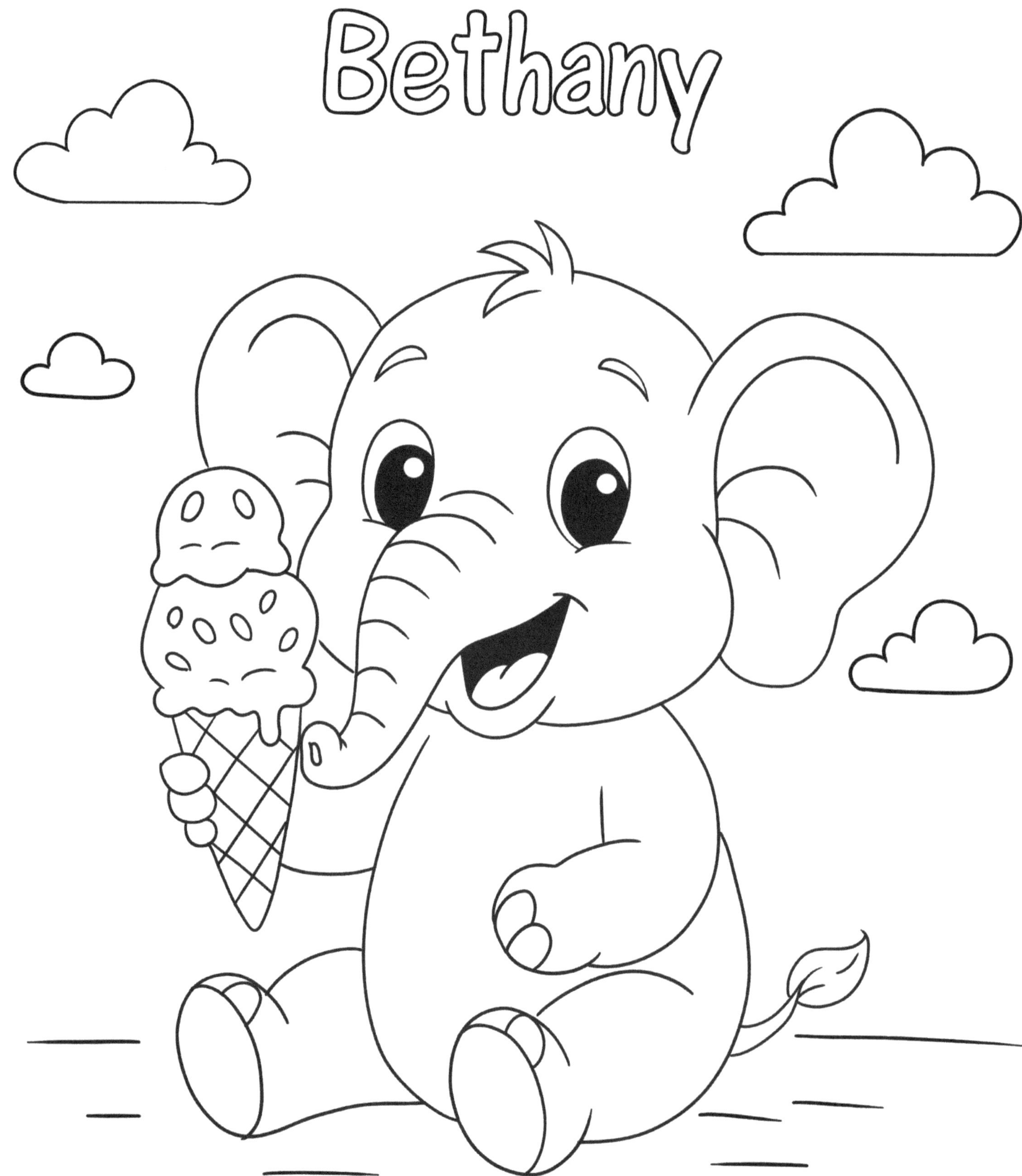

Bethany

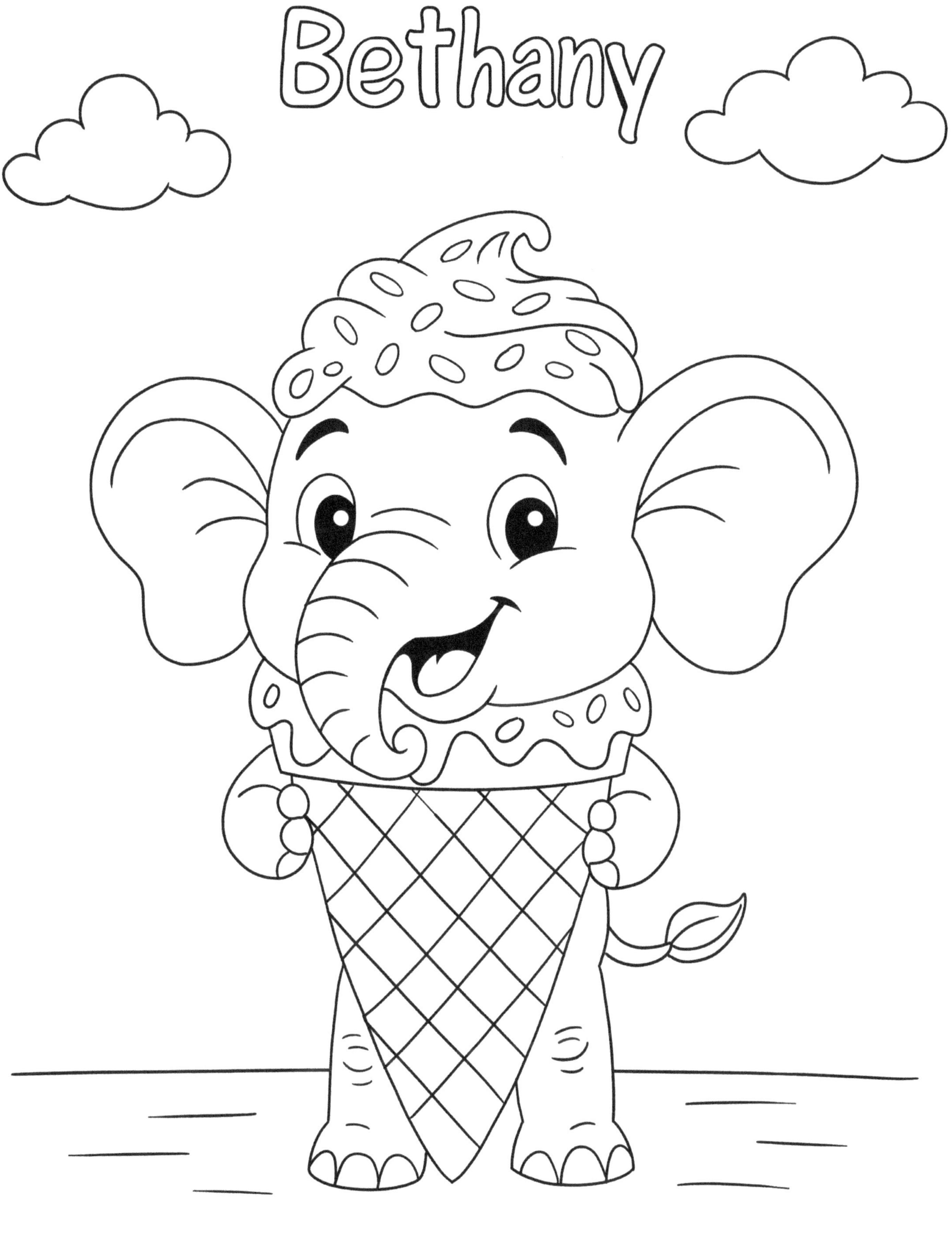

Bethany

Owen

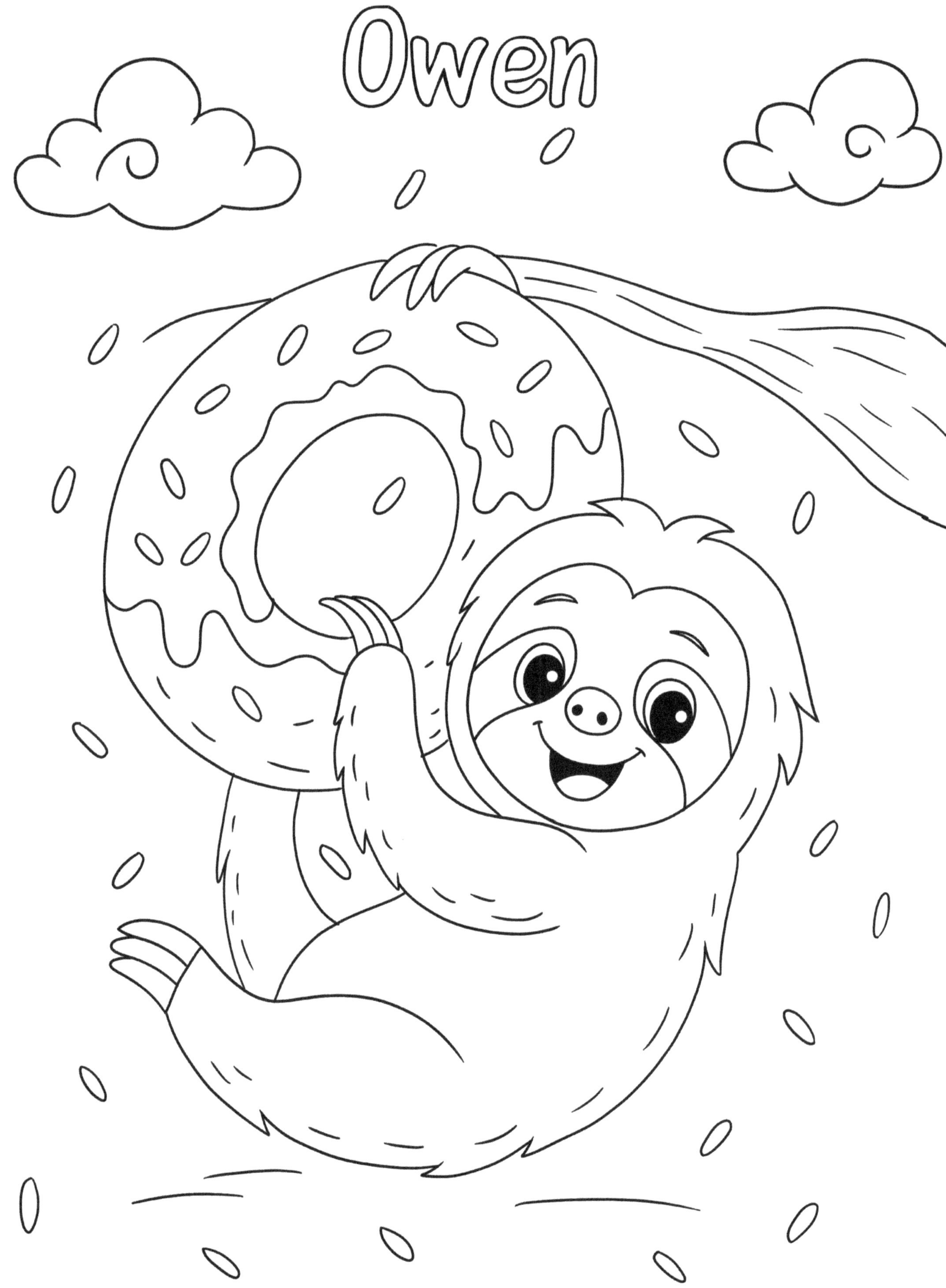

Owen

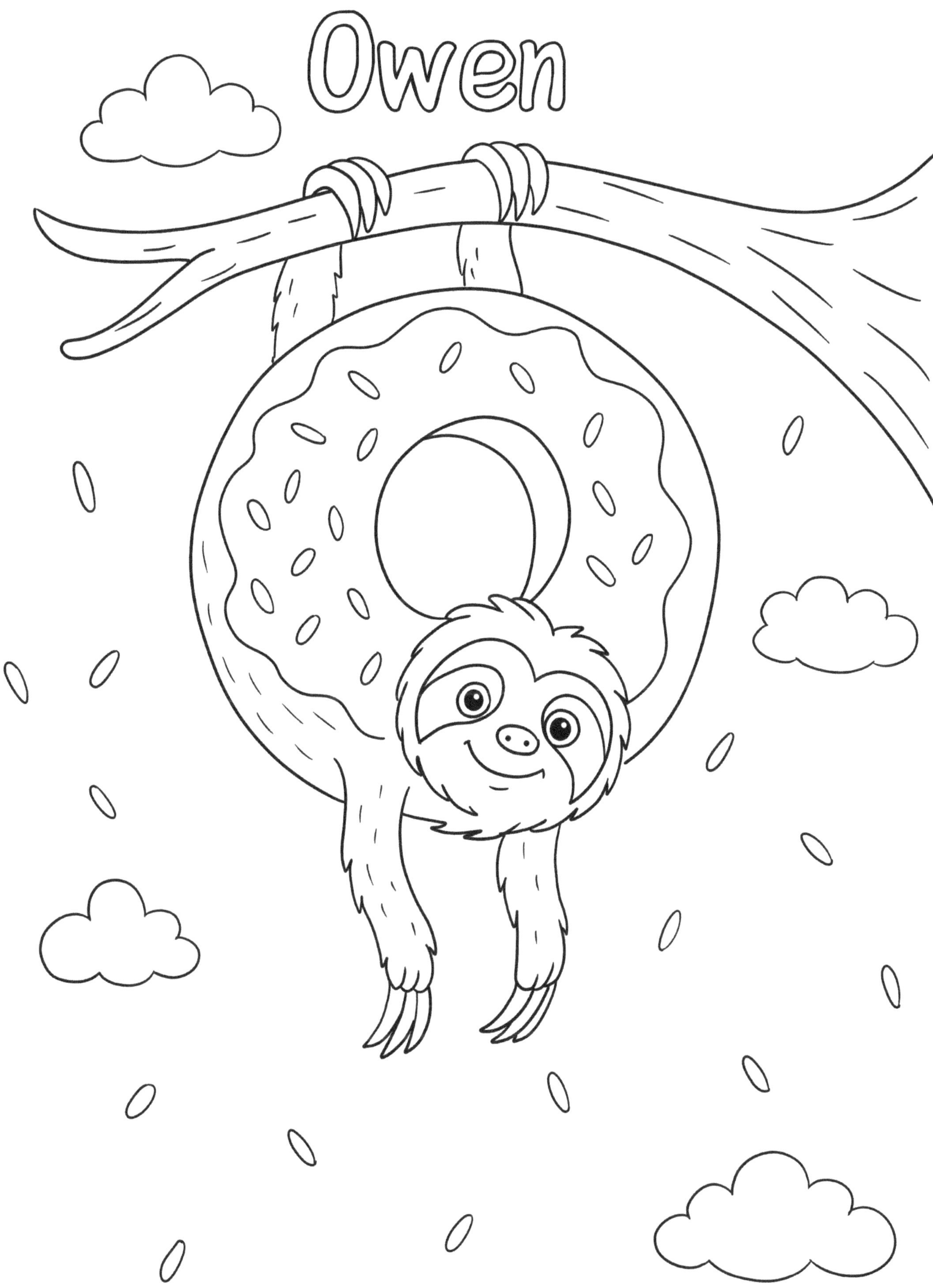

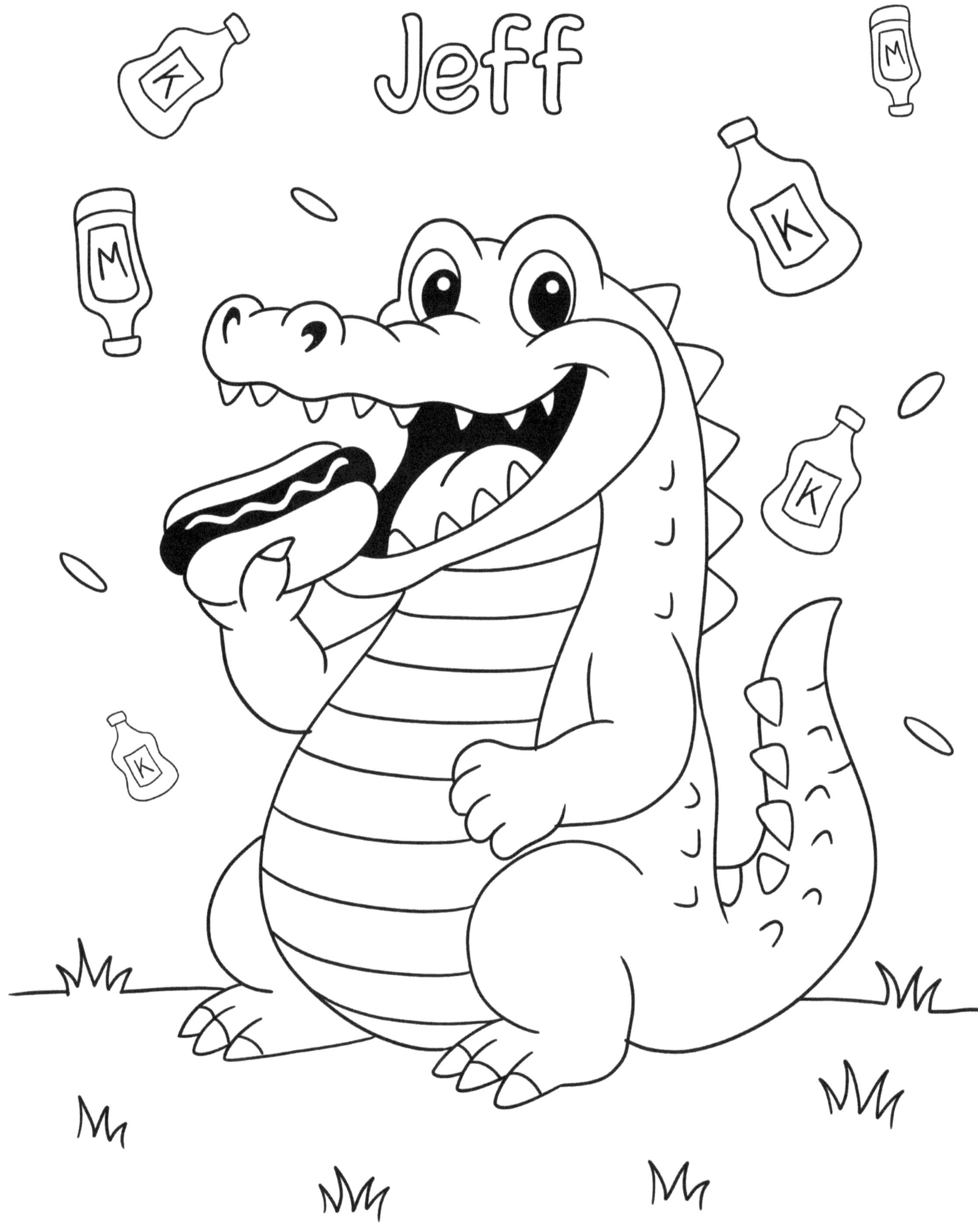
Jeff

Jeff

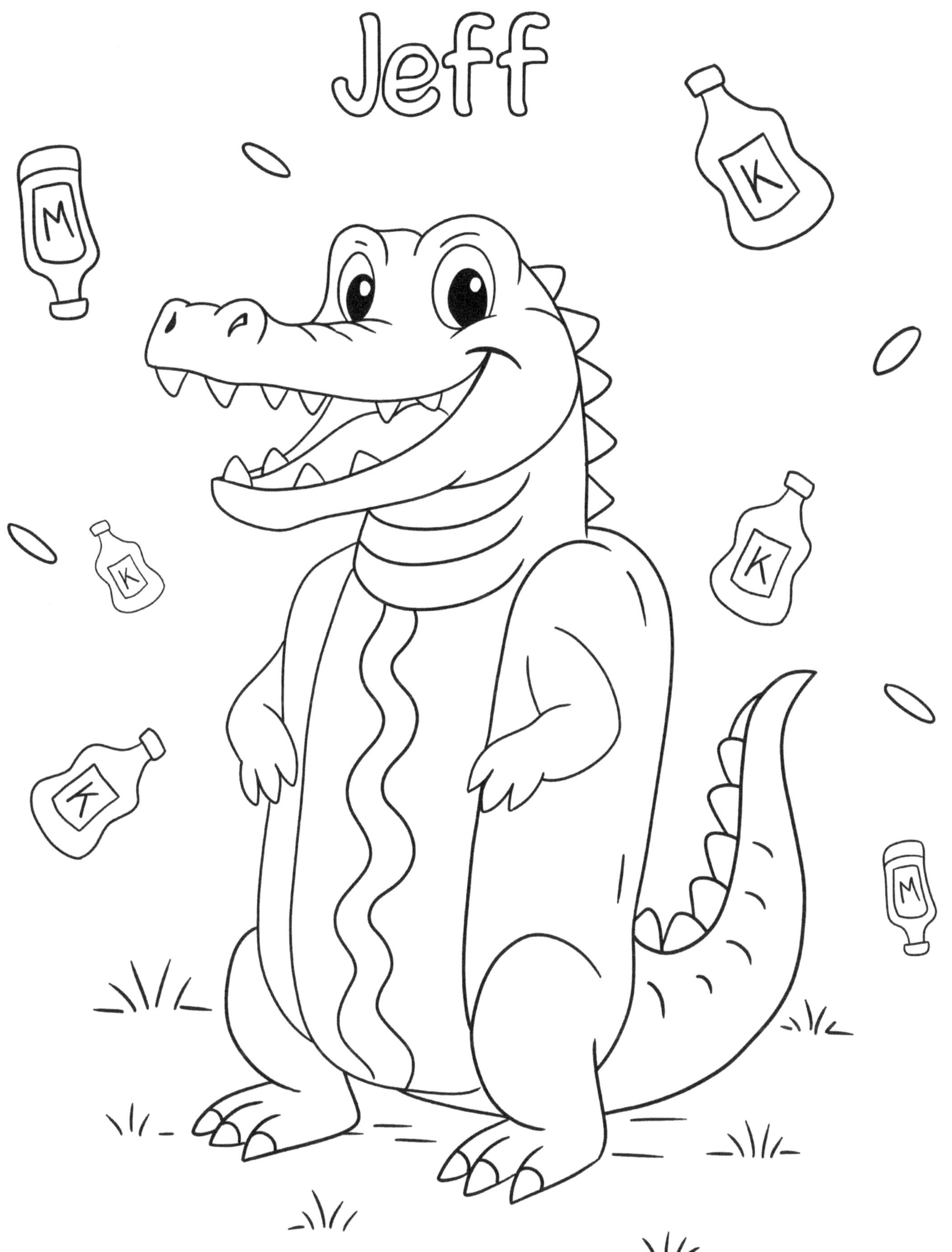

Grace

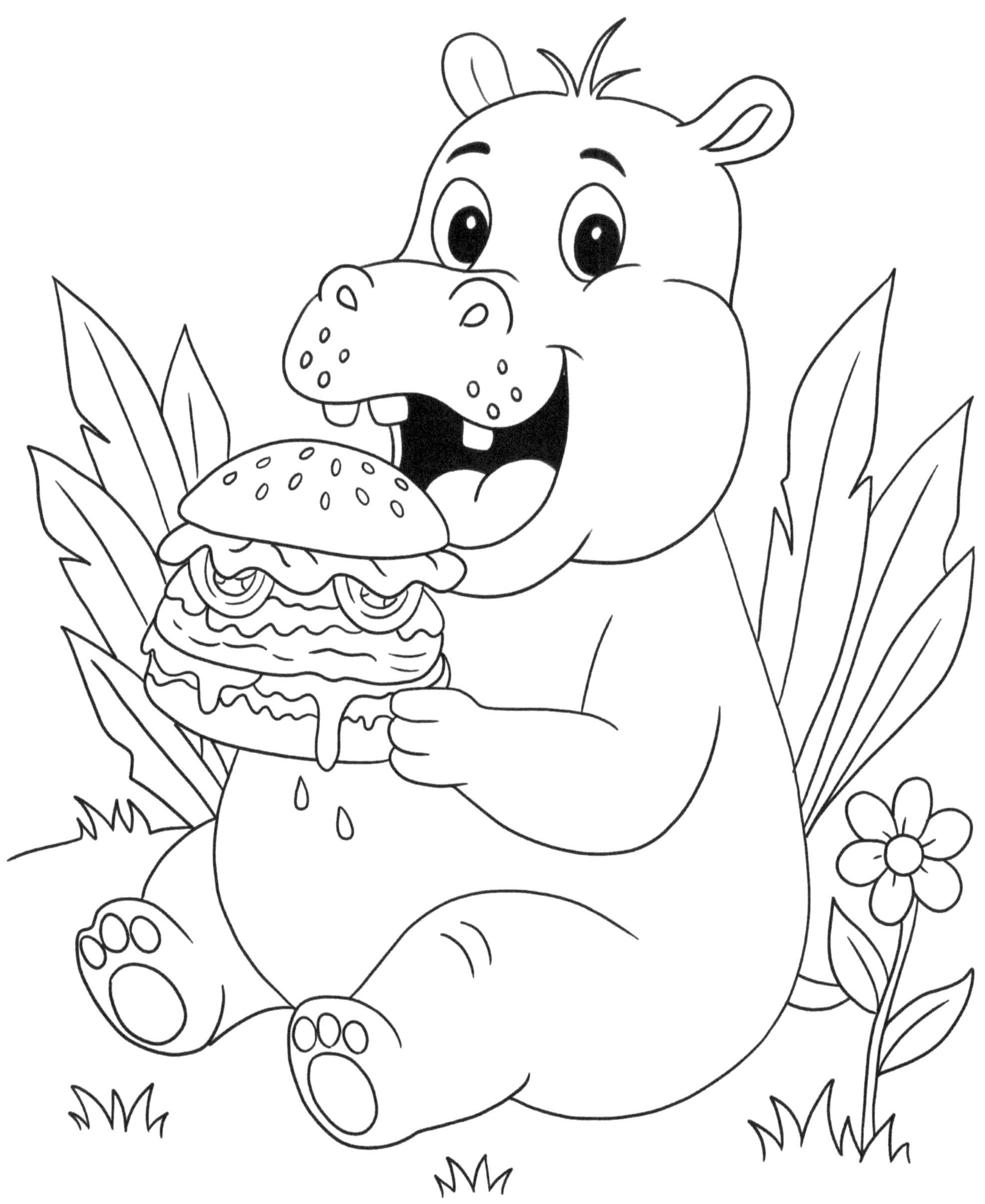

Grace

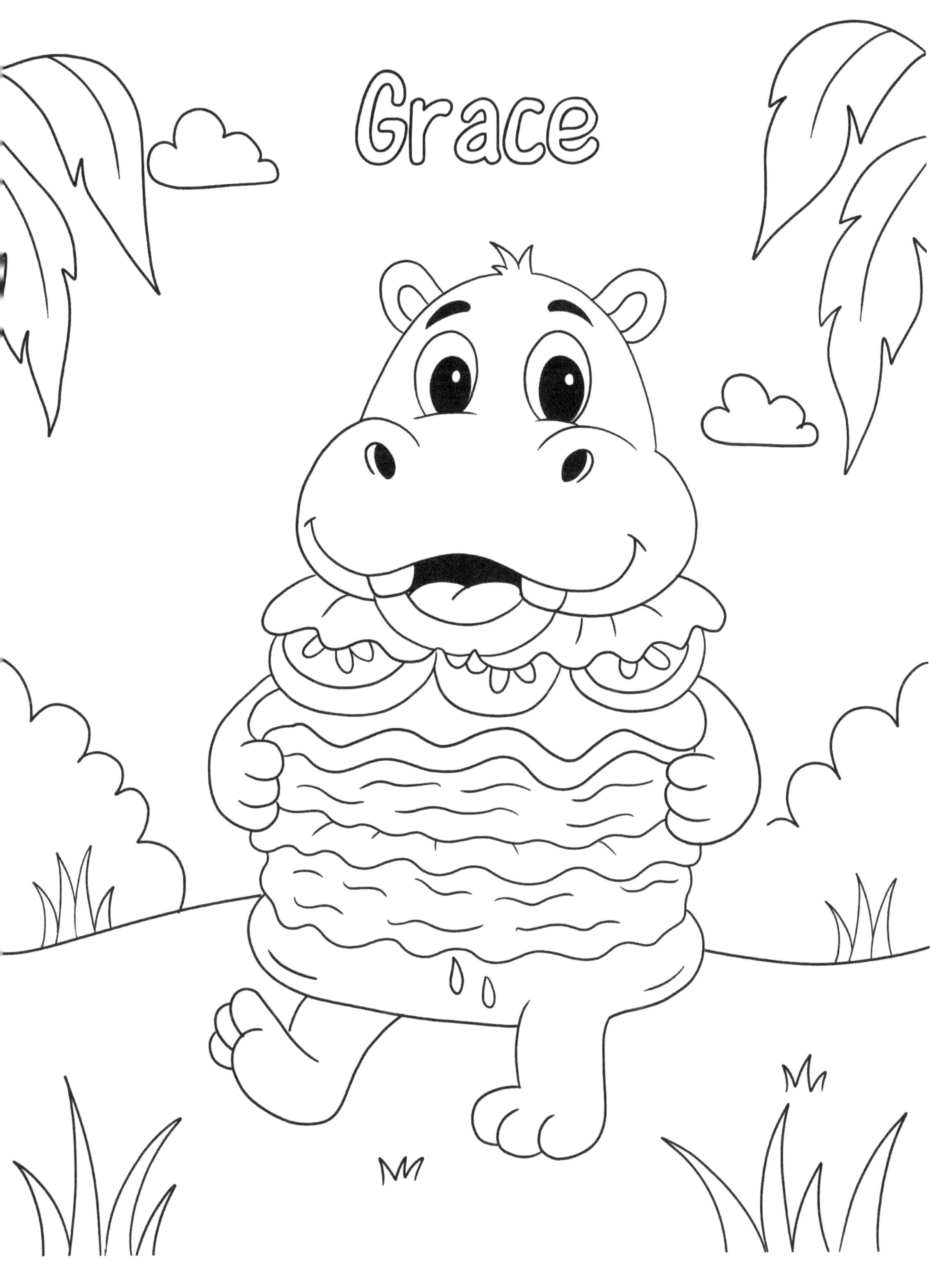

Emma

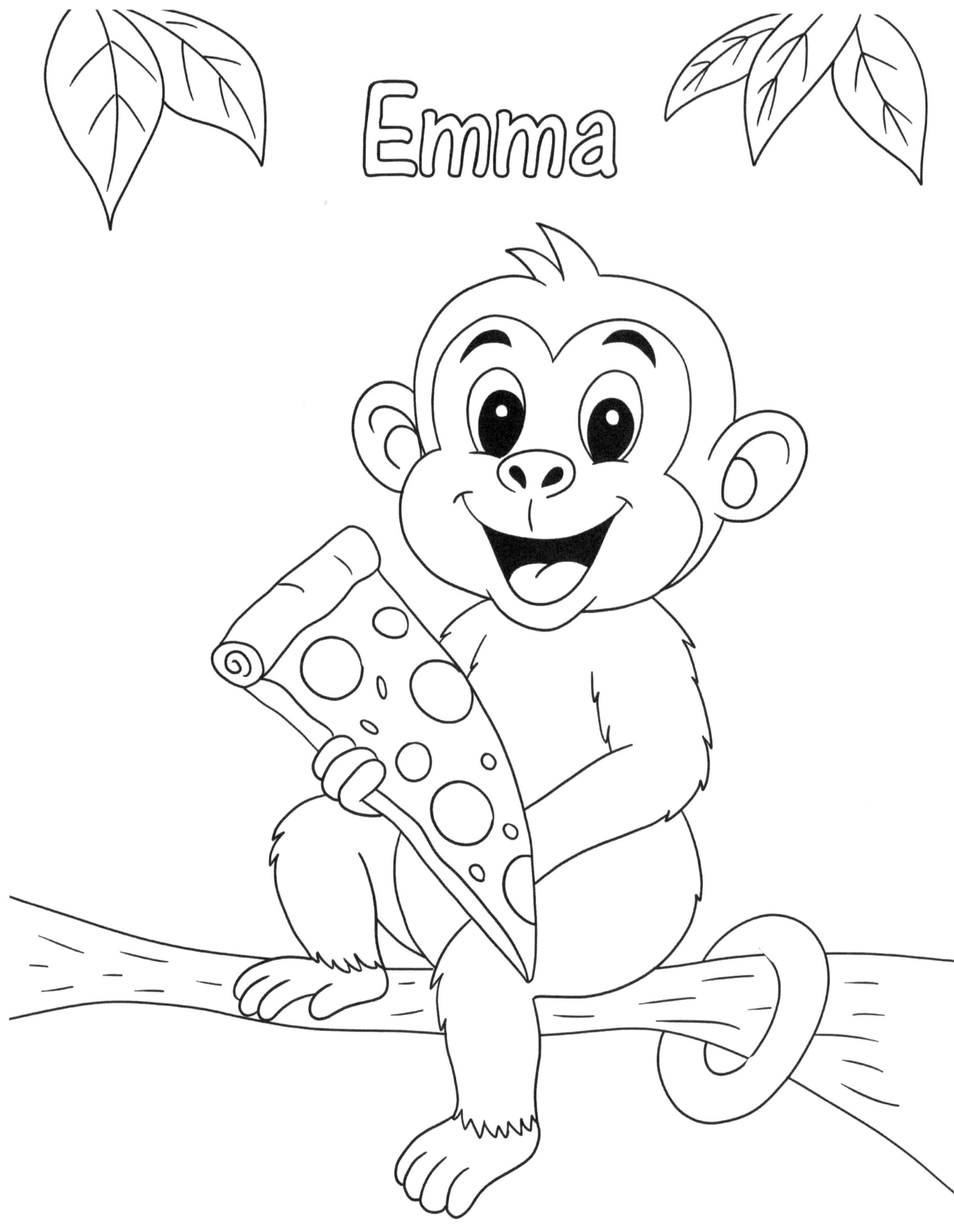

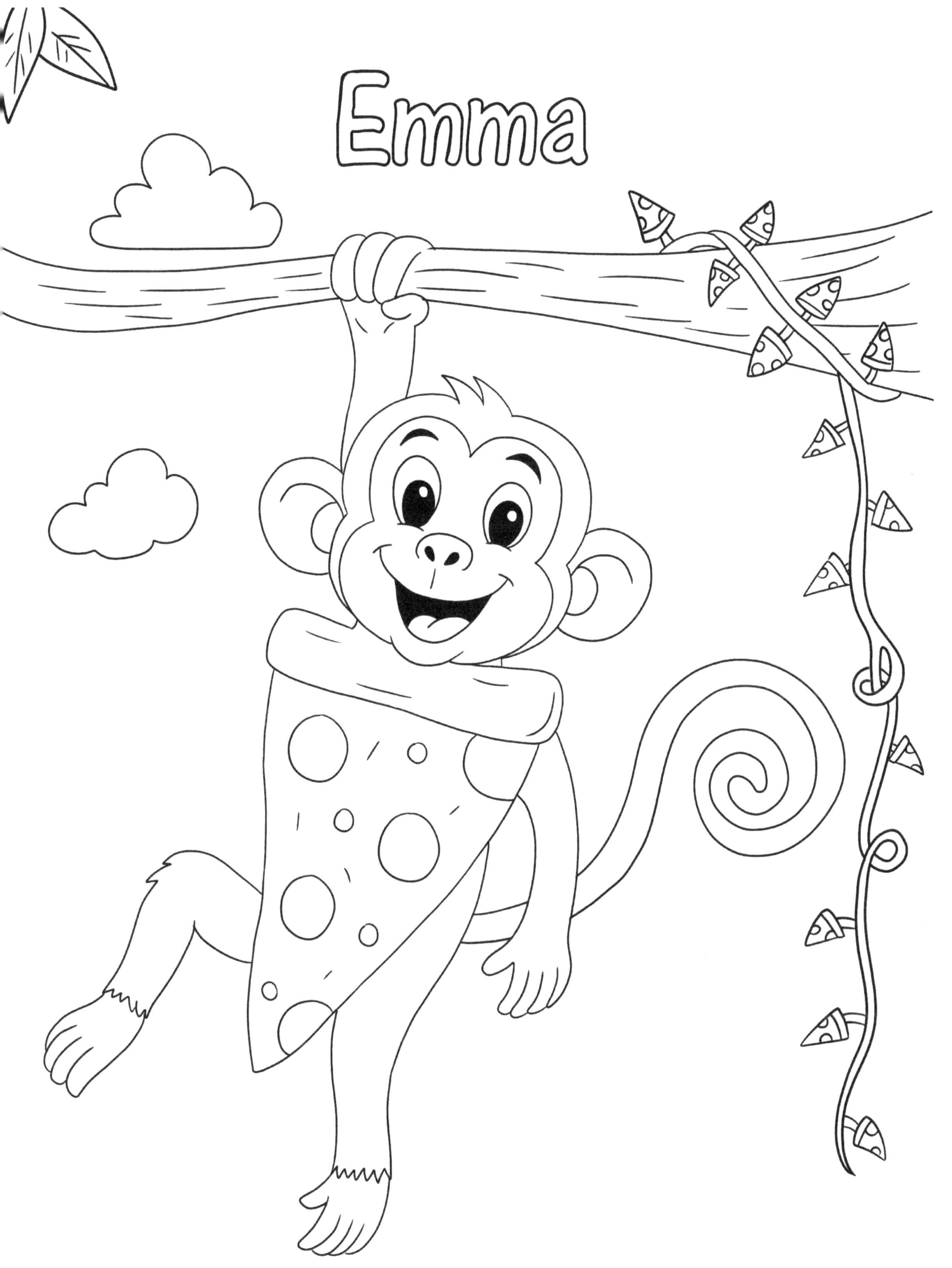
Emma

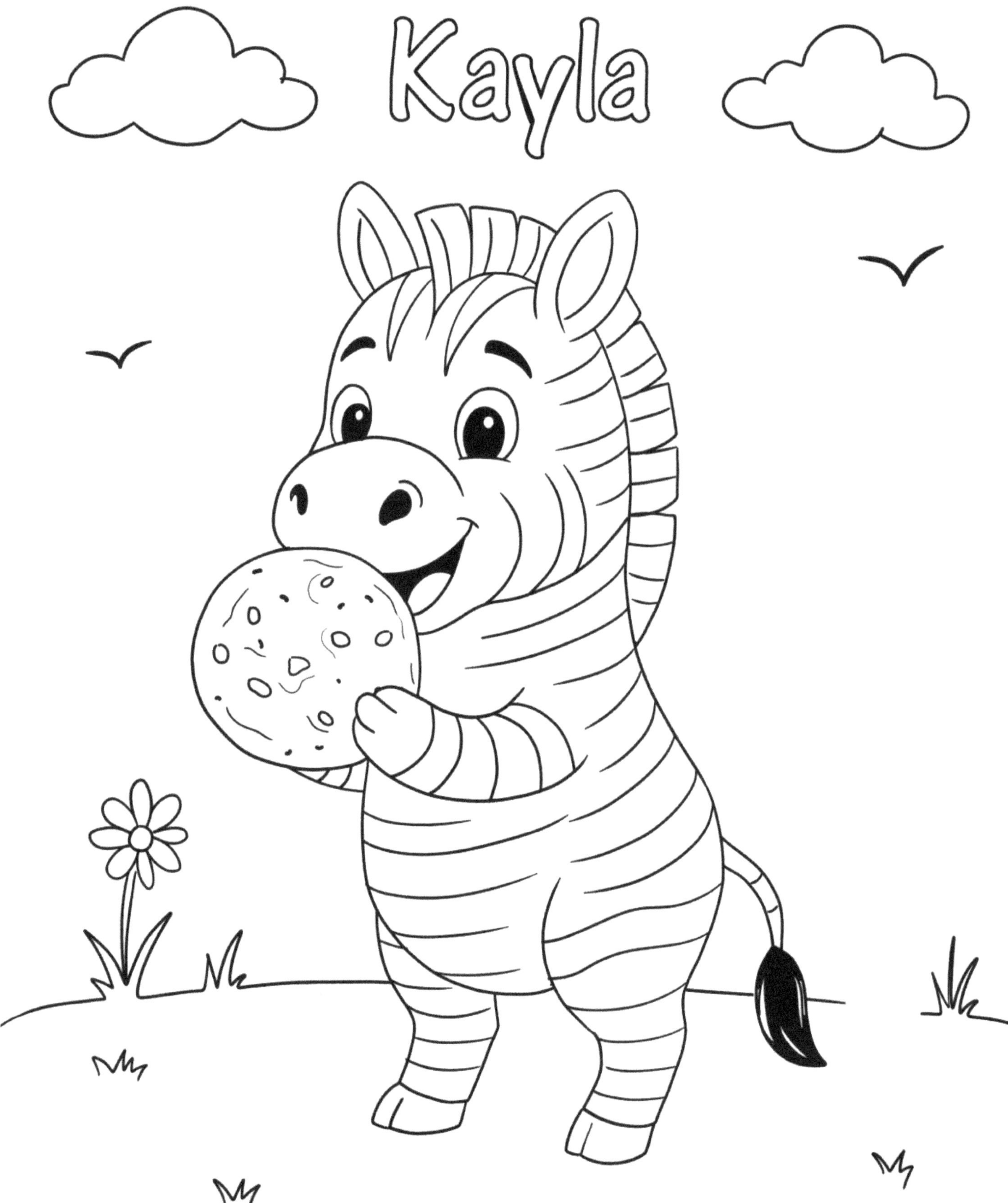
Kayla

Kayla

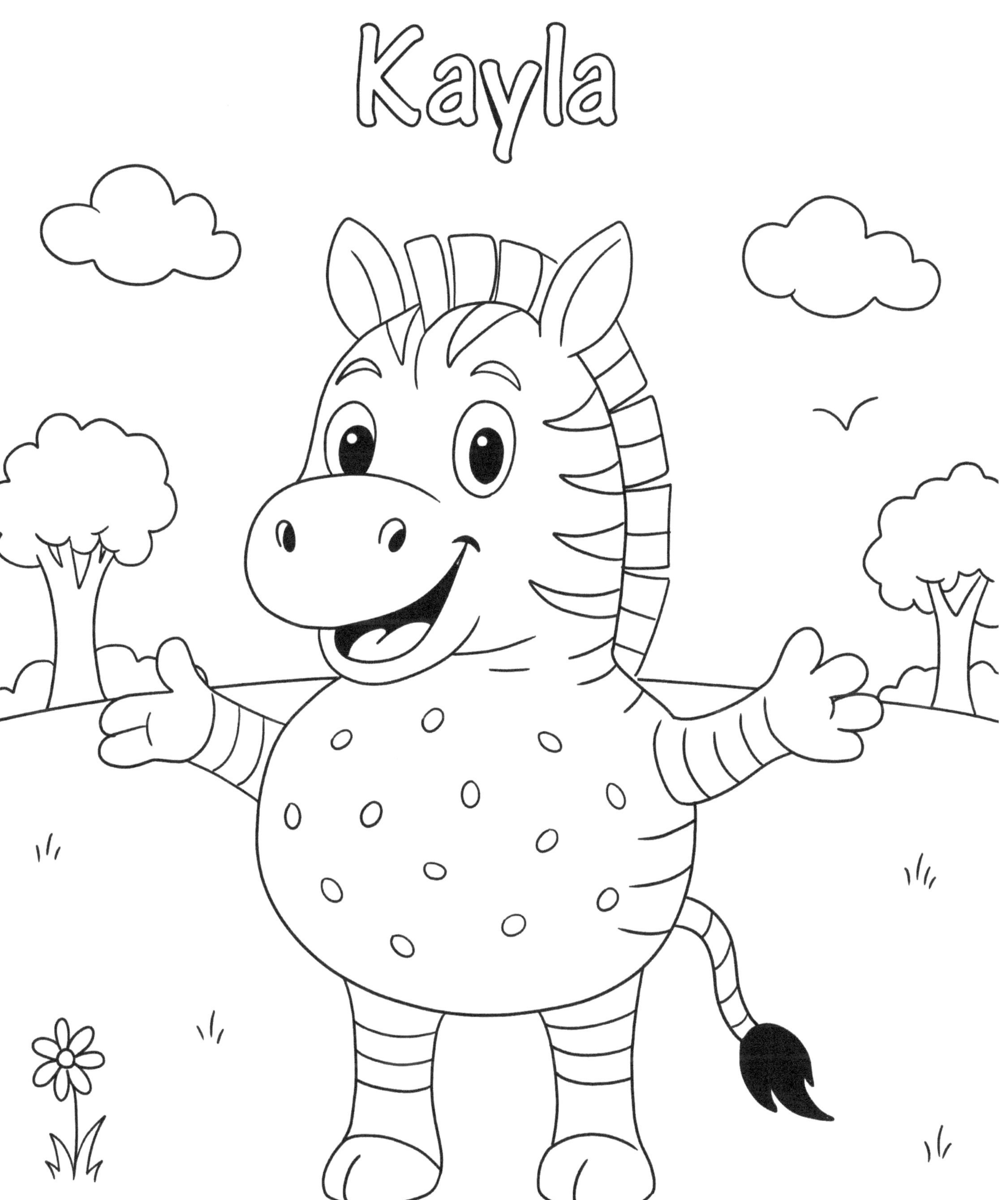

Candace

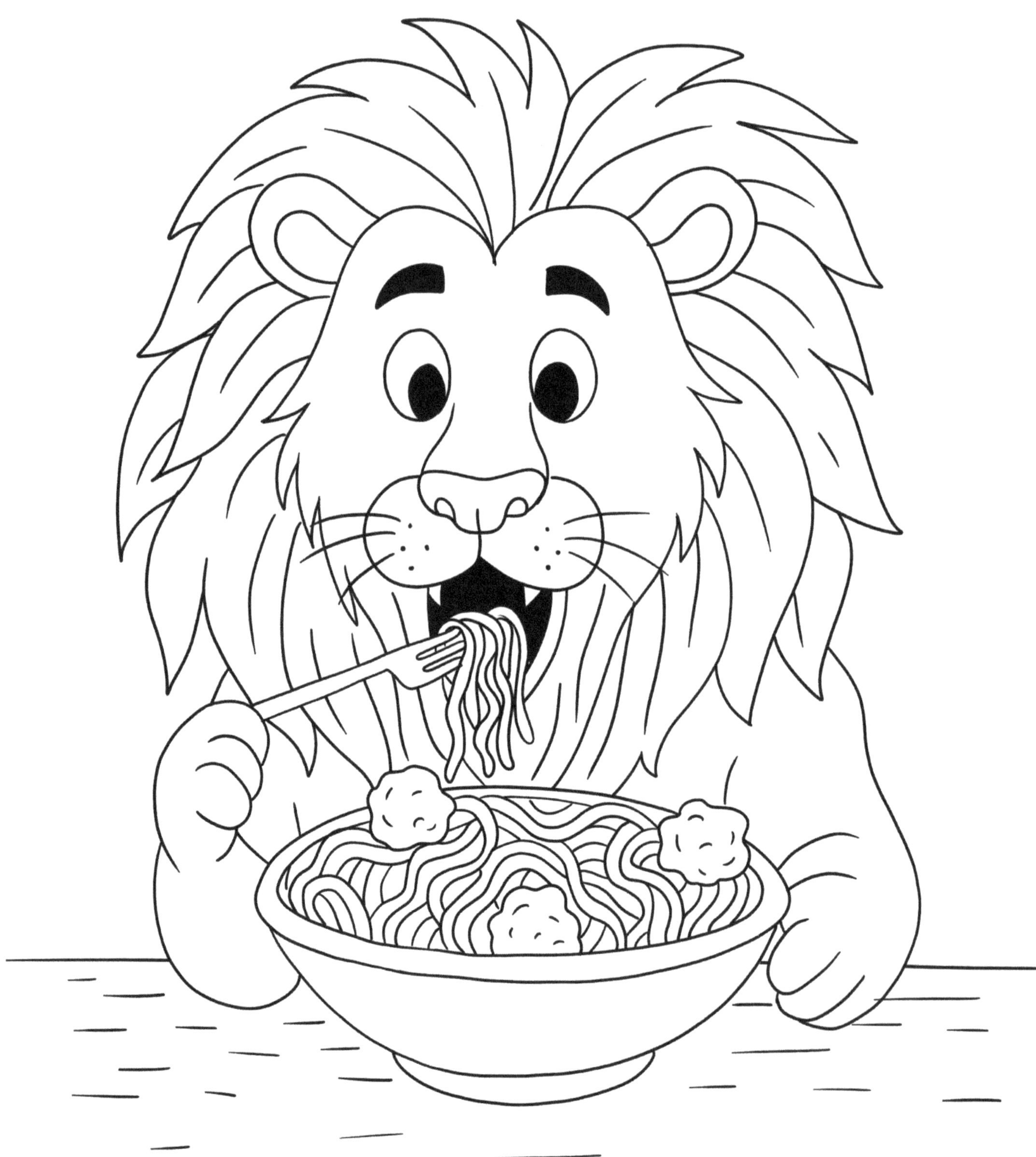

Candace

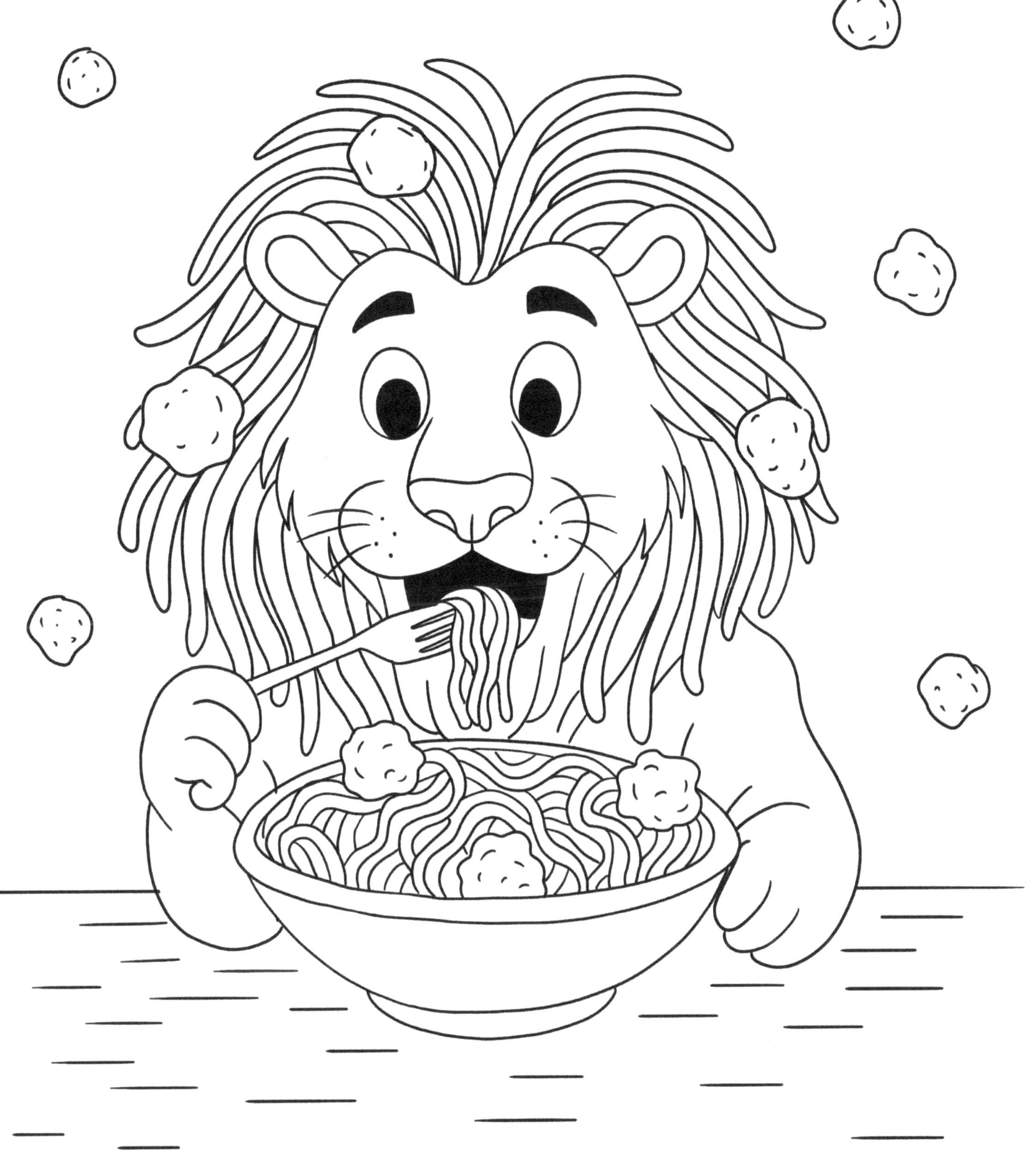

Landon

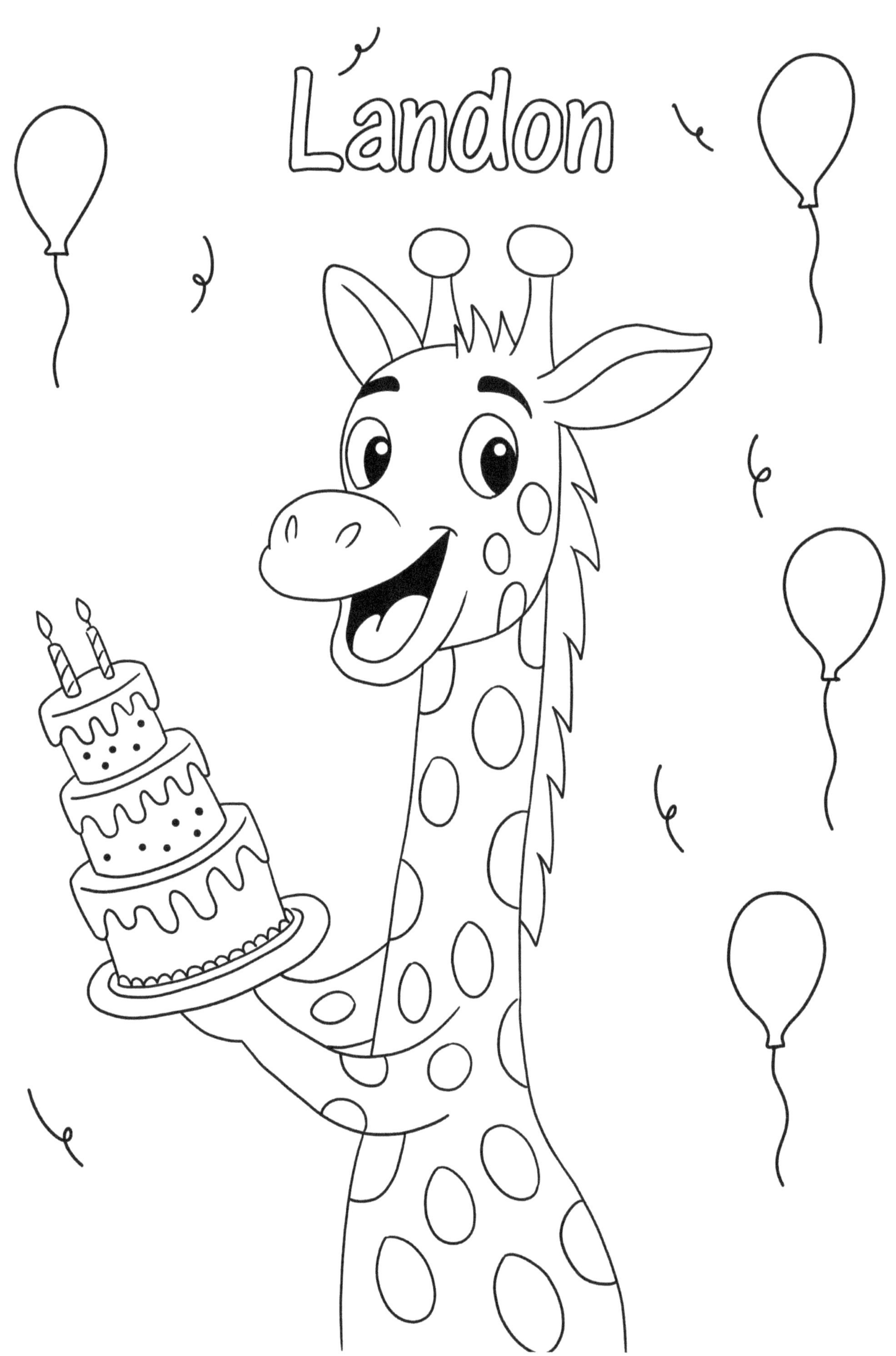

Landon

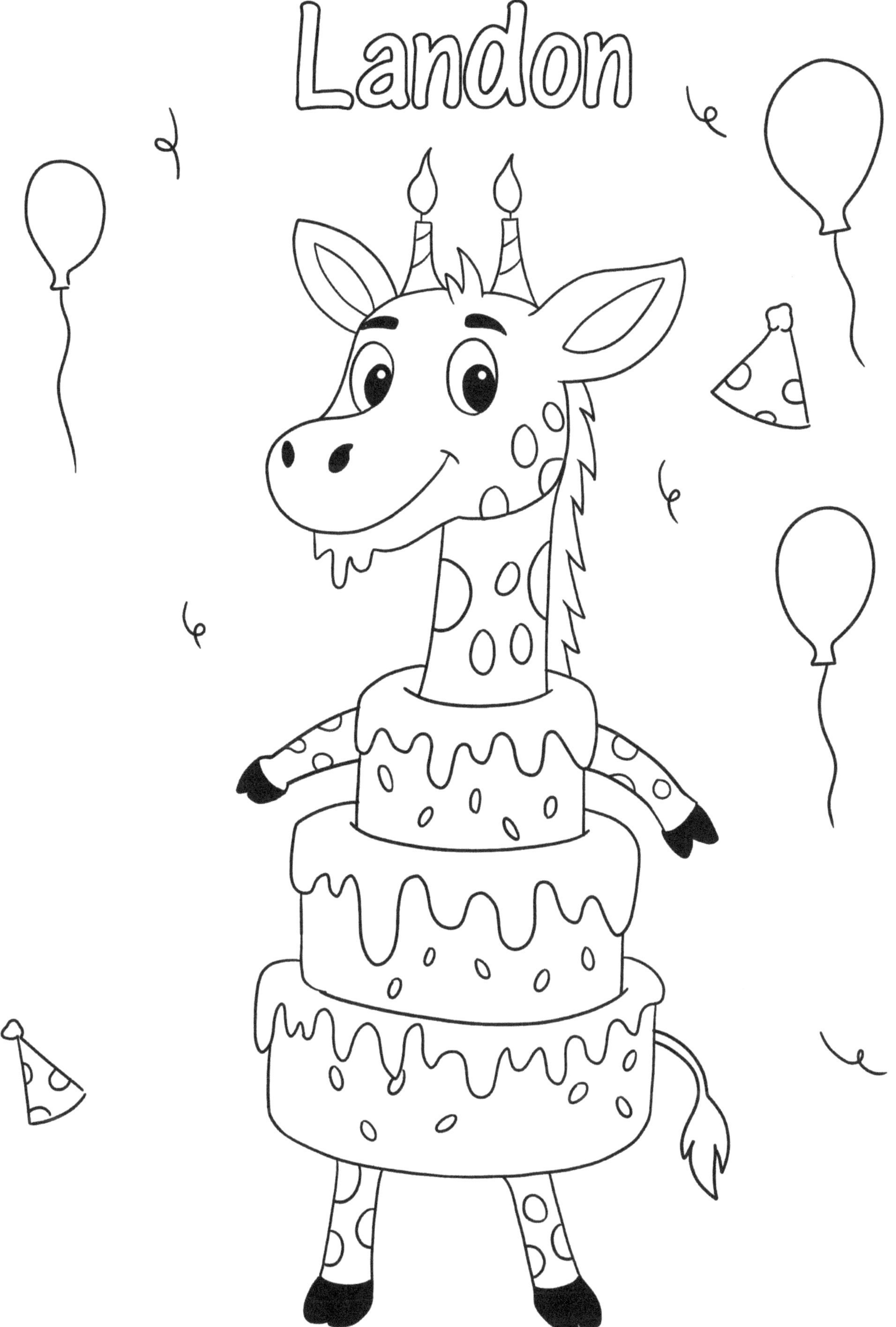

Finn

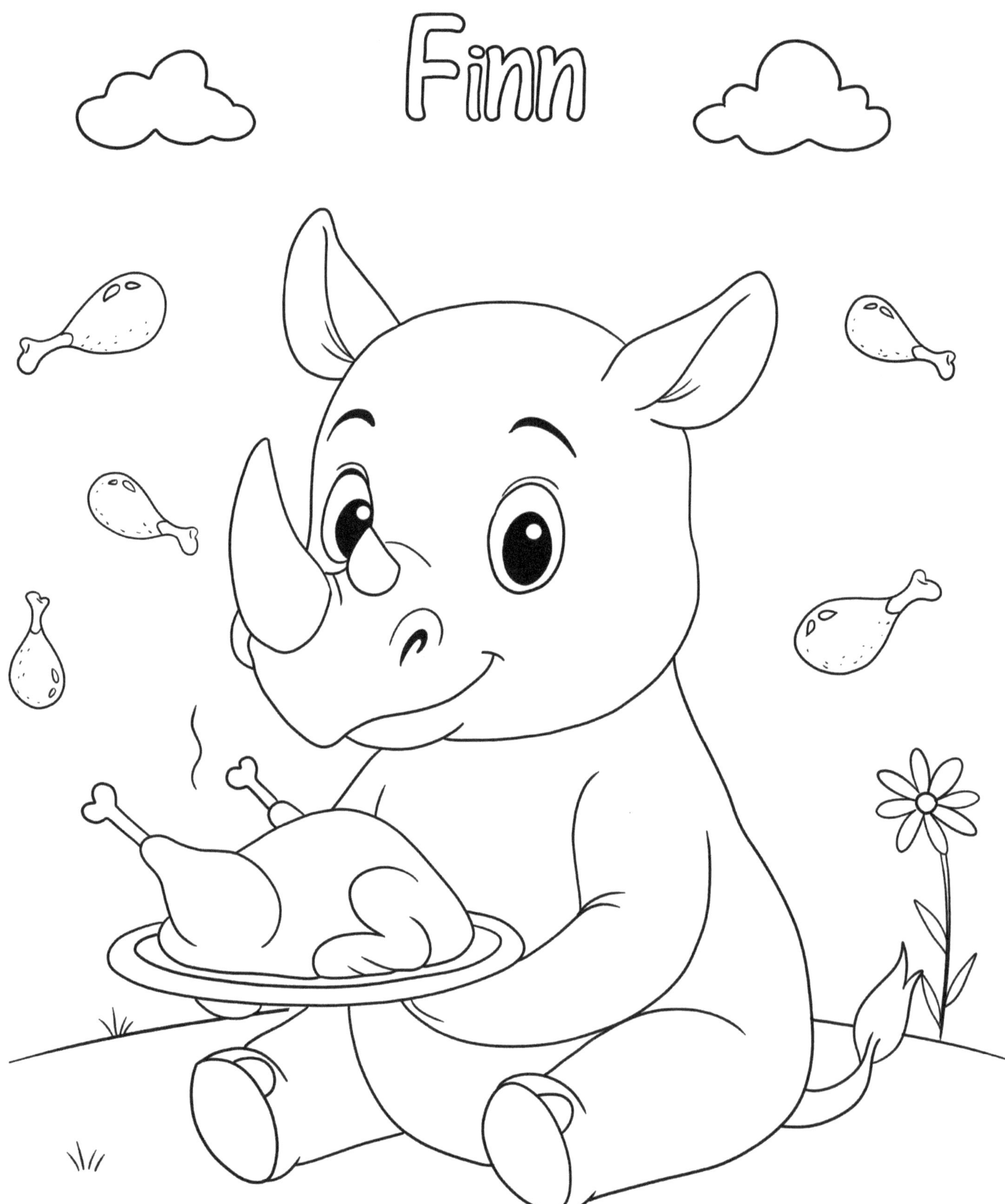

Finn

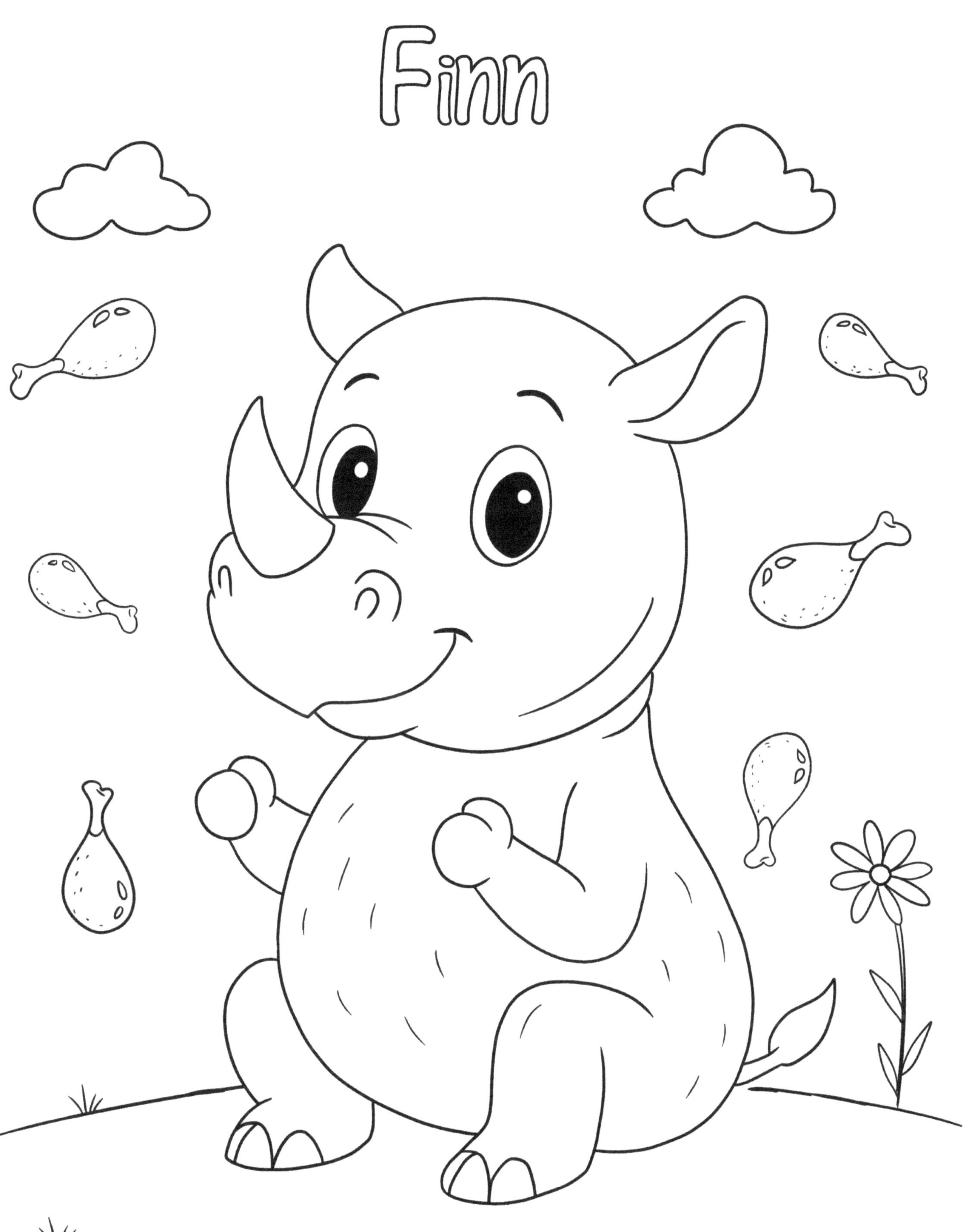

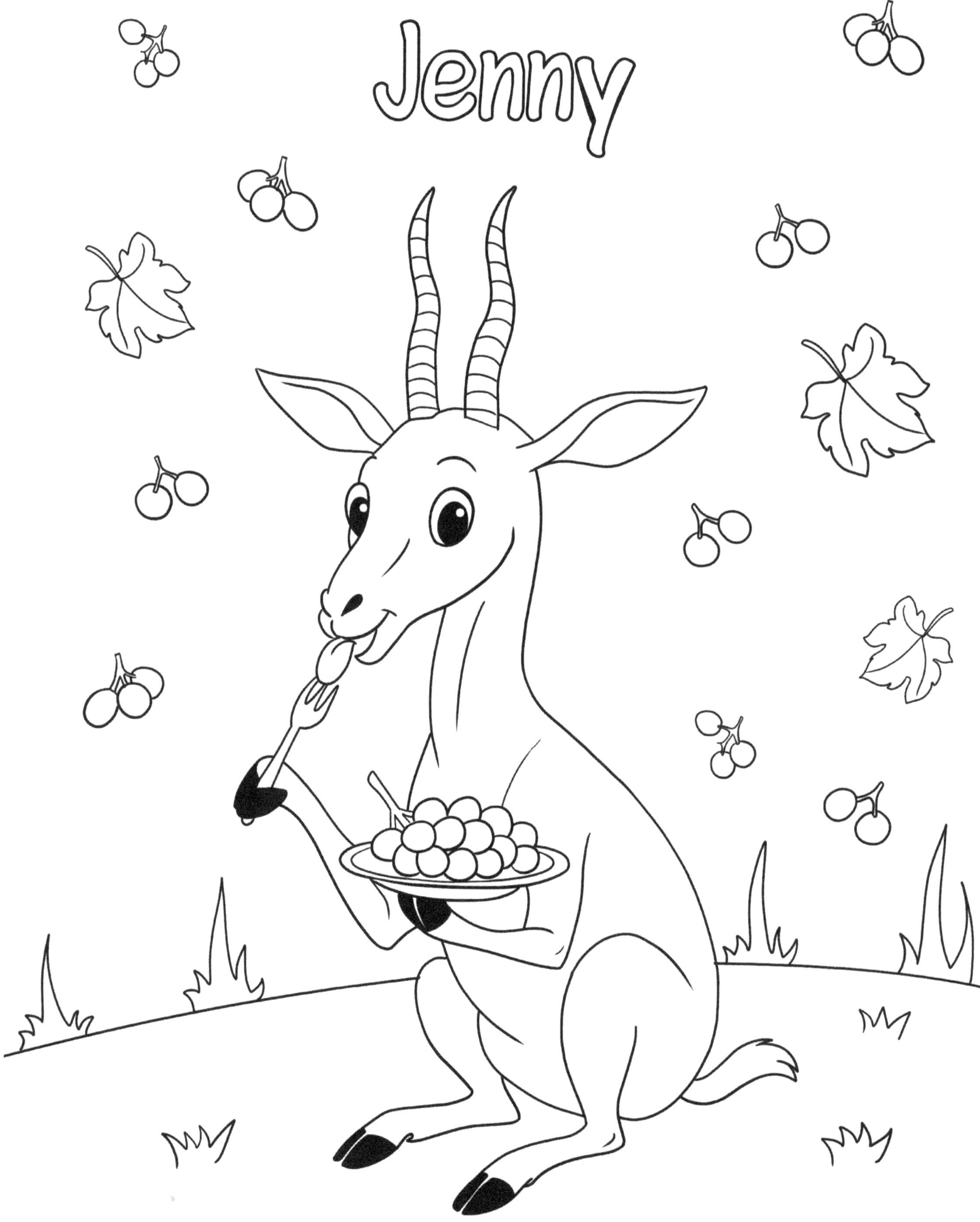

Jenny

Jenny

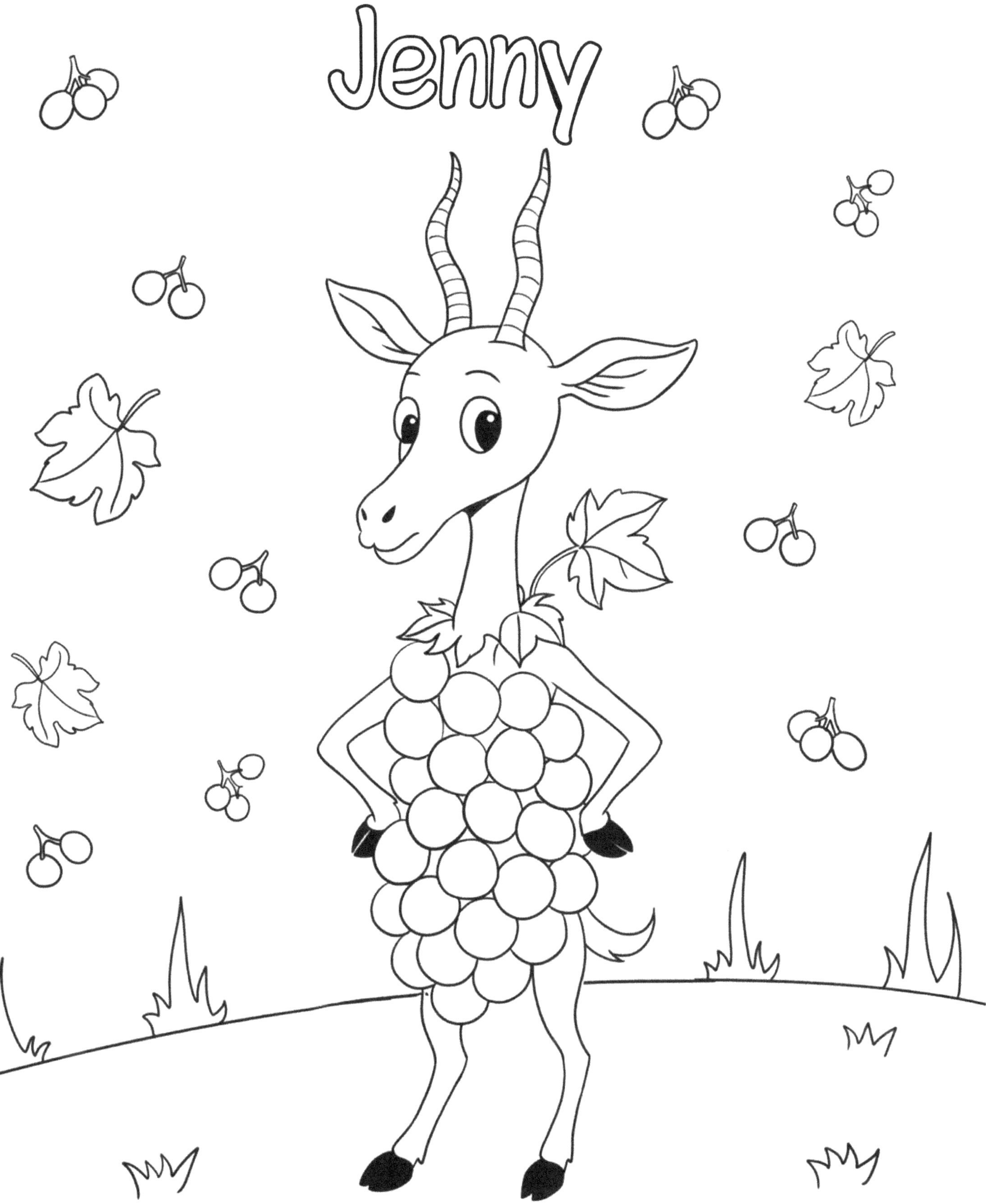

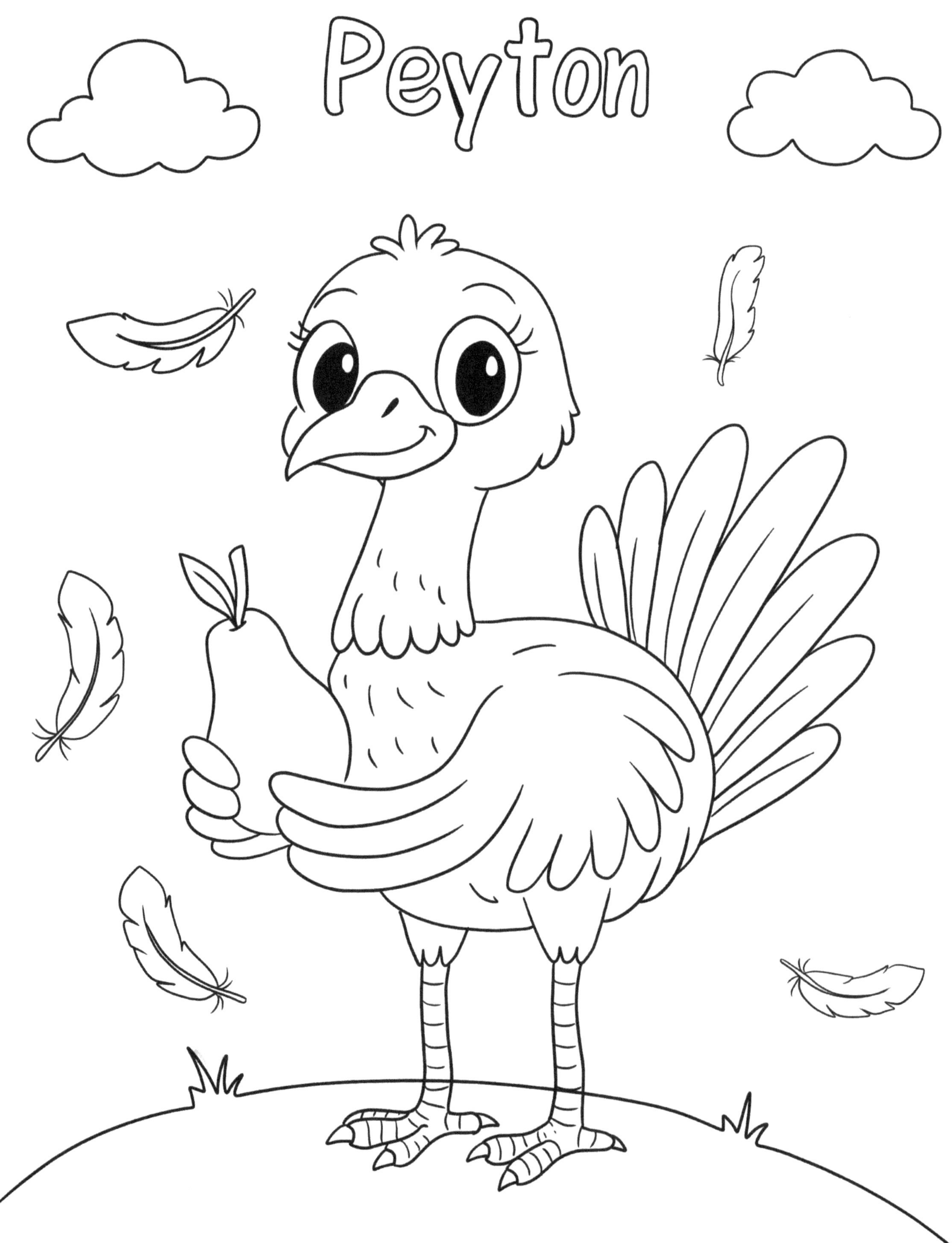

Peyton

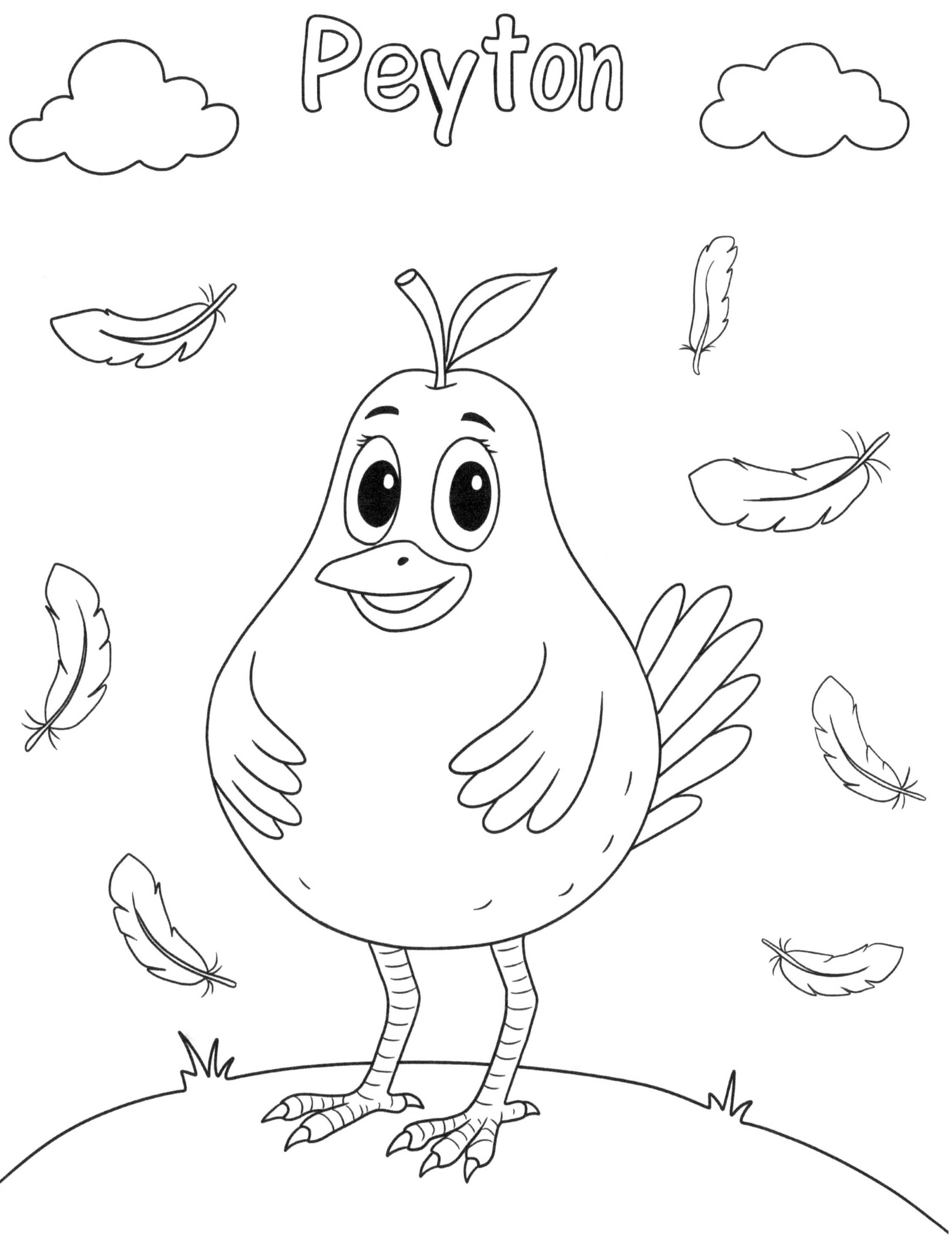
Peyton

Layne

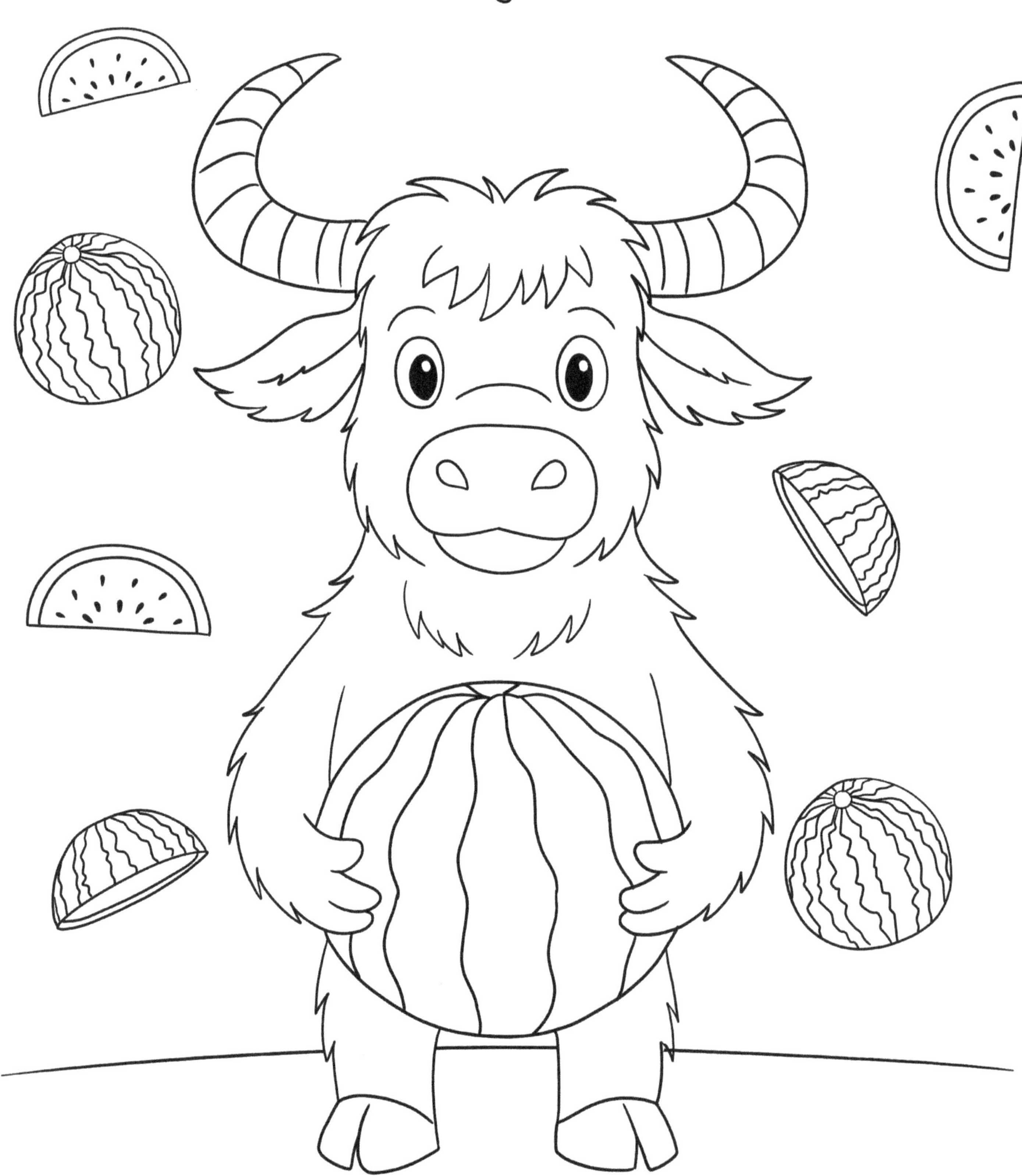

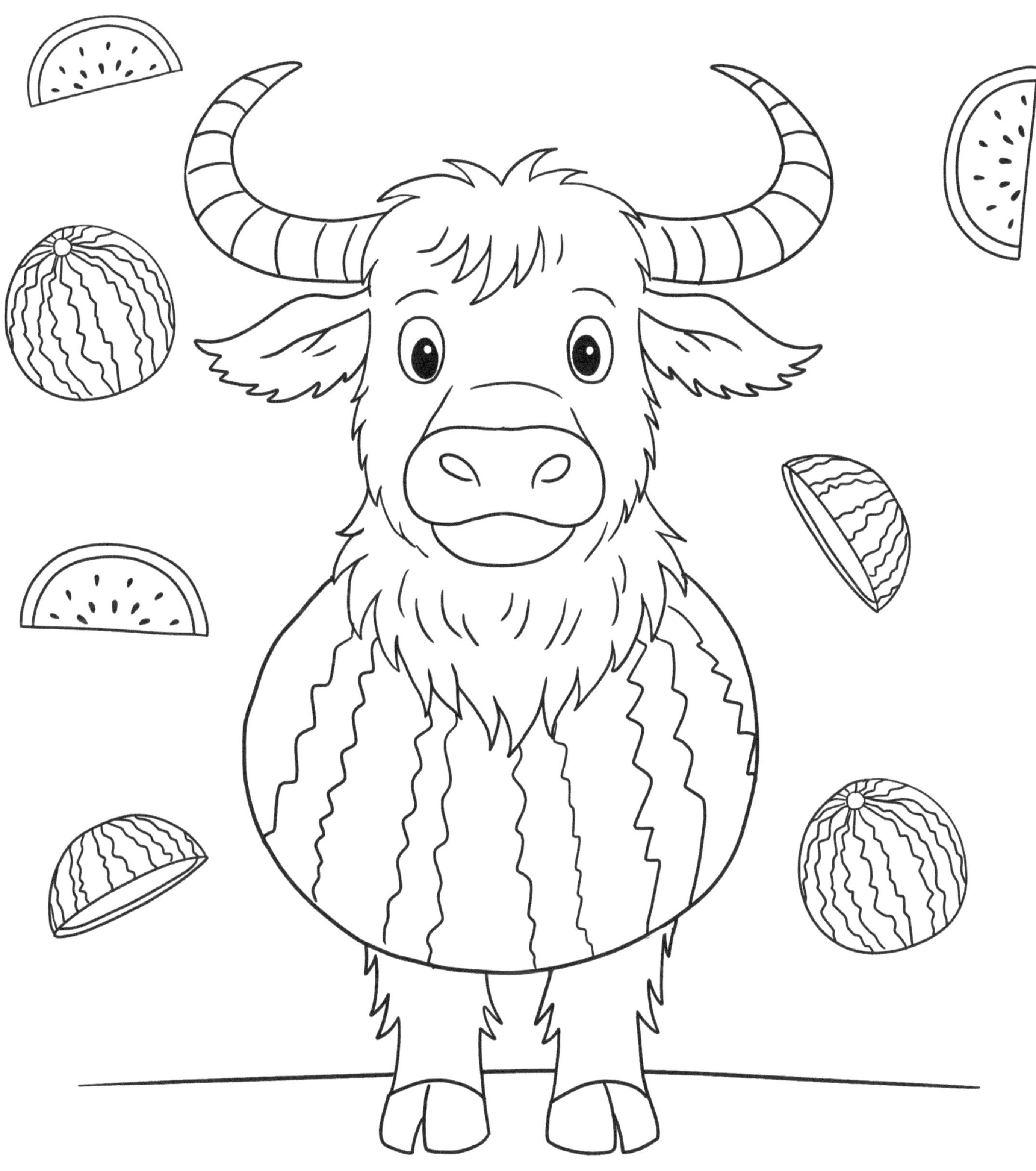

Layne

Help Emma find her pizza

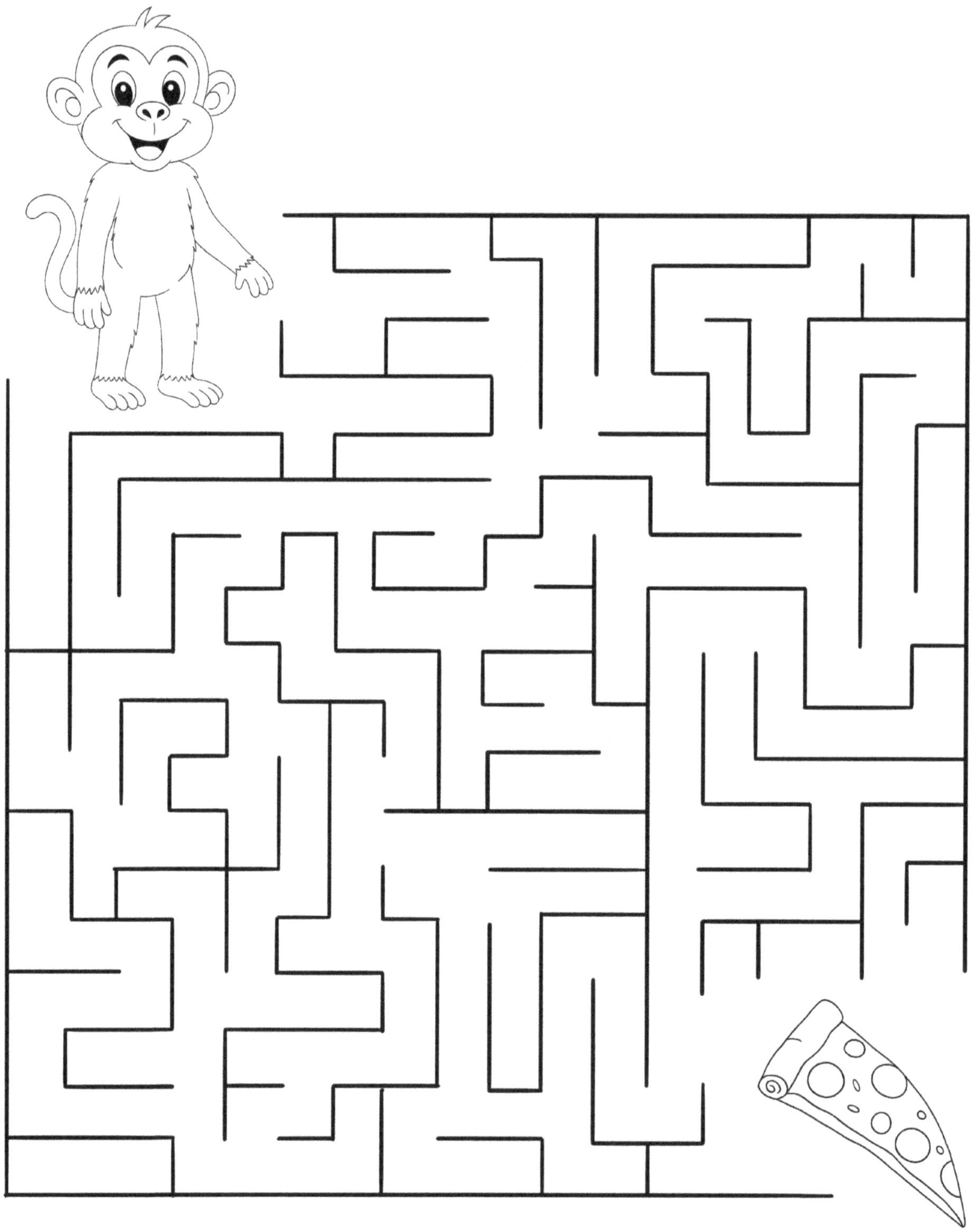

Match Animal to Food

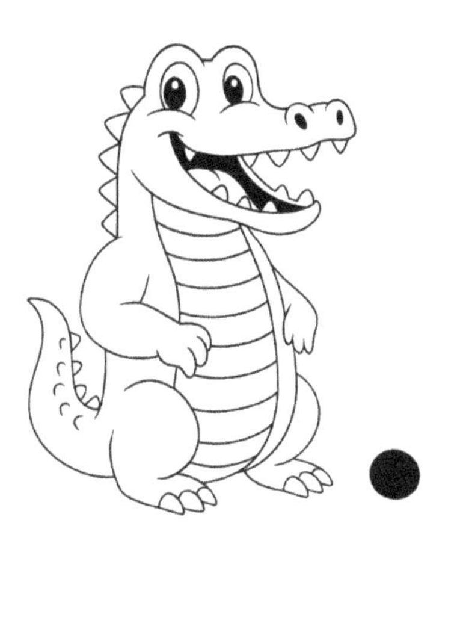 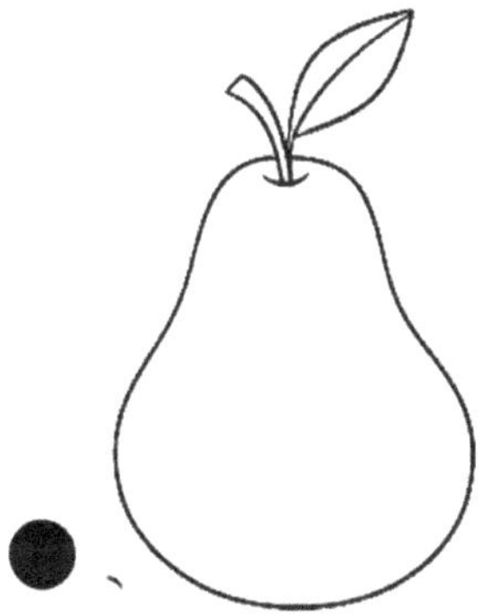

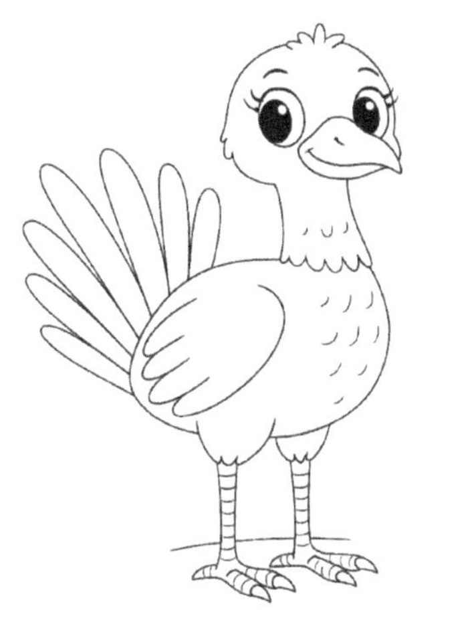 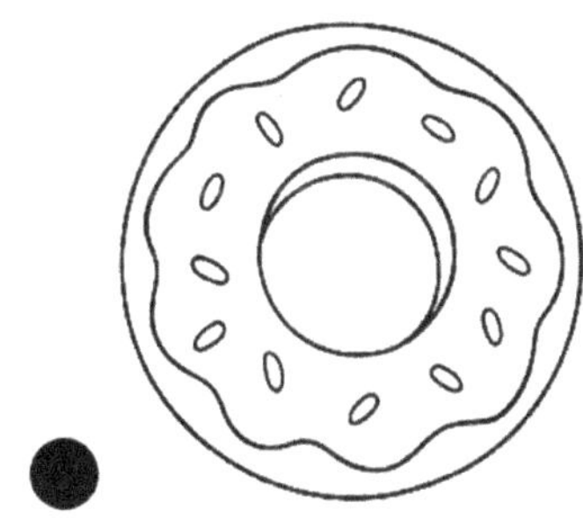

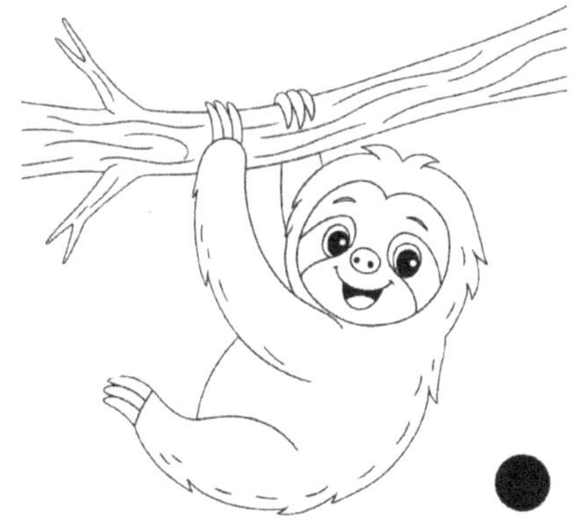 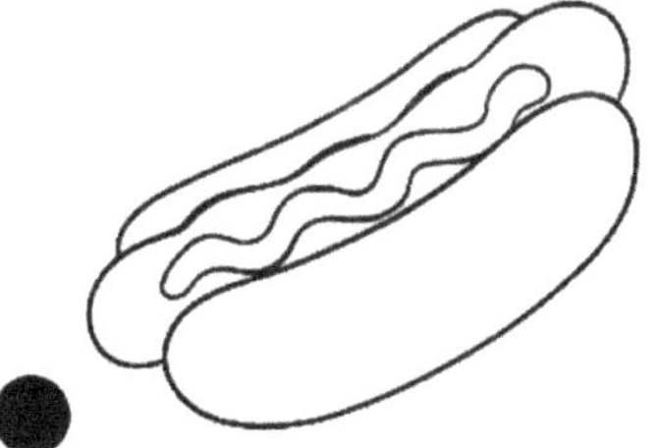

Spot the Difference

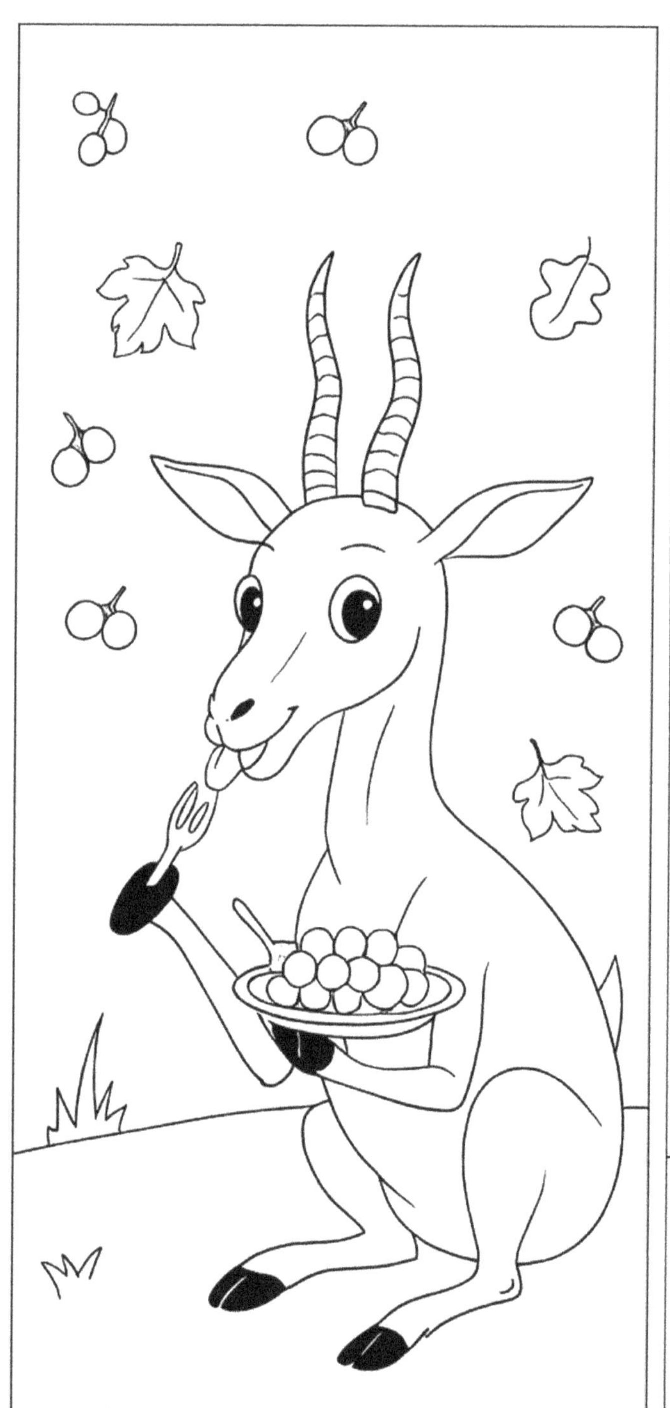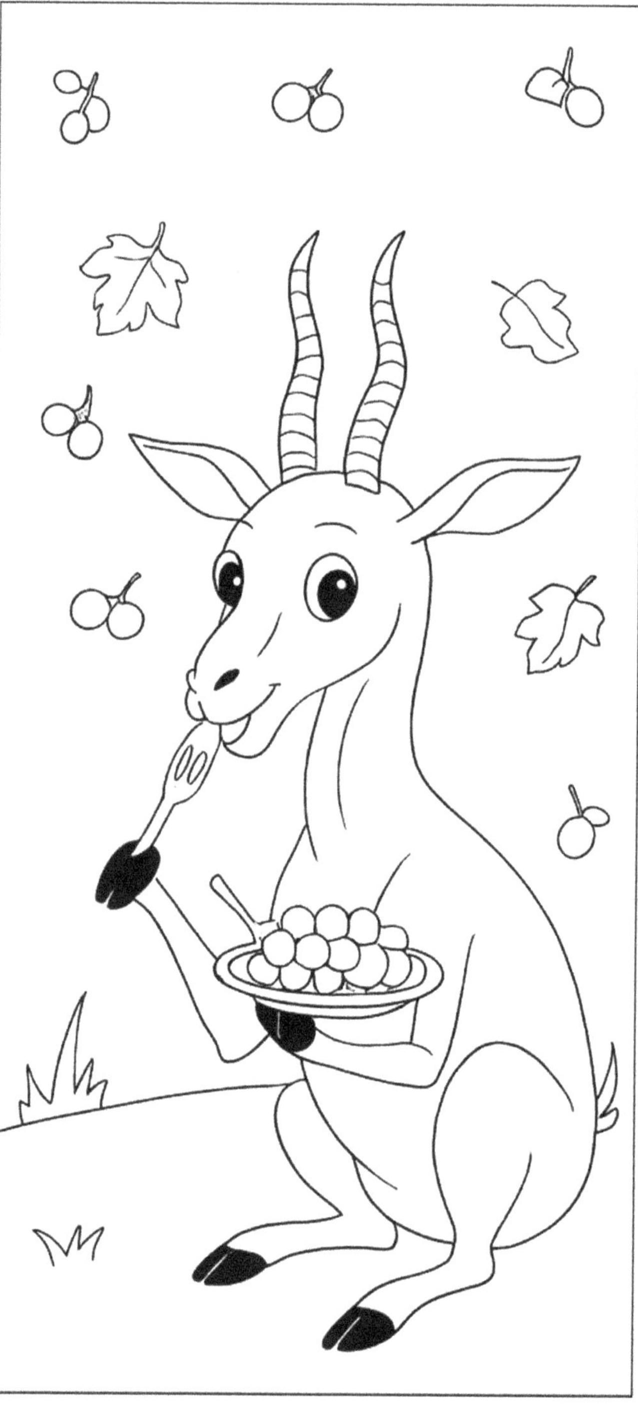

Draw your Animal eating
a crazy Food

Color the Animals

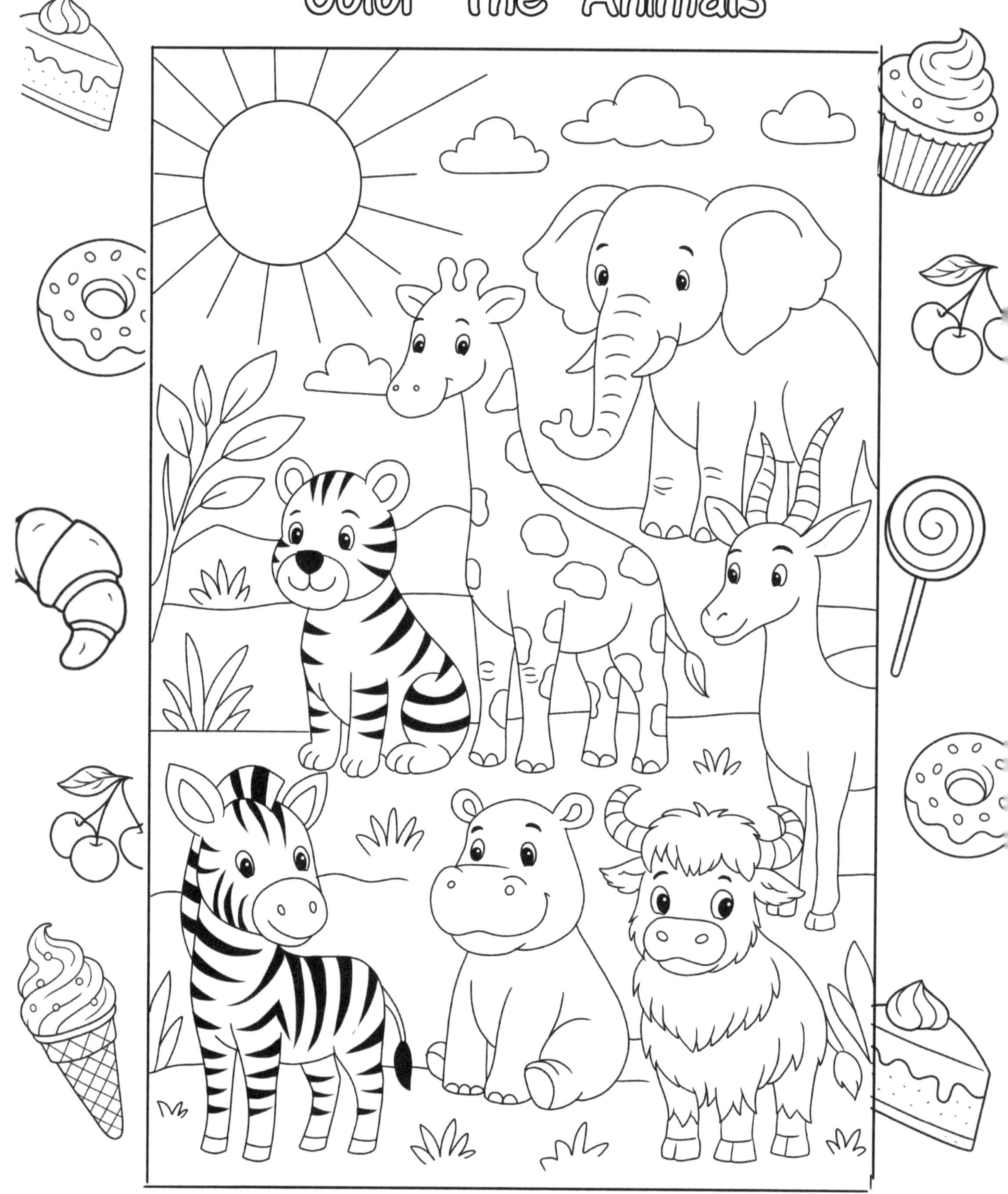